What's Under the Sea?

What's Under

the Sea?

Solveig Paulson Russell

illustrated by
Nancy Gugelman Johnstone

Abingdon
Nashville

What's Under the Sea?

Library of Congress Cataloging in Publication Data

RUSSELL, SOLVEIG PAULSON.
What's under the sea?
Includes index.
Summary: Examines characteristics of the ocean including the currents, tides, floor, and plant and animal life.
1. Ocean—Juvenile literature. [1. Ocean. 2. Marine biology] I. Title.
GC21.5.R87   551.46   81-20521   AACR2
ISBN 0-687-44913-8

To April Kristen Metcalf, who lives by the sea, and whose inquiring mind is always ready to grasp new meanings.

CONTENTS

INTRODUCTION

When you stand on the beach and look out at the sea, there's nothing but water to be seen. Water stretches out on every side and goes on farther than your eyes can see. The water is always moving, making waves and foam, and running up to the land at the ocean's edge.

If we stand at the ocean's edge, we can look down and see the sand under the edges of water that lap the beach. But we can't see what's under the water even when we are a short distance out. What is the water hiding? How does it look down under the moving waves? What's under the sea?

The Vastness of the Seas

When we look over an ocean we are lost in wonder at its great size. Yet what we see is only a tiny speck of all the oceans of the world. Together the oceans of the world cover more than 141 million square miles, or more than two thirds of the earth's whole surface.

There are four great oceans. The largest is the Pacific Ocean, the second in size is the Atlantic, the third largest in size is the Indian Ocean, and the next largest is the Arctic. These four bodies of water have smaller seas and gulfs. They make up a vast chain of water that completely circles the earth.

Changes in Sea Level

The land masses of earth as they look today—the continents and islands—were not always as our maps show them now. Many thousands of years ago some of the land masses were connected with one another. The sea water did not separate them, but dry land, called land bridges, joined together the masses.

Scientists have discovered that the level of the oceans change slowly over long periods of time. Parts of the edges of continents, or large areas of long-ago land, are now under water. And some parts that were once under water are now above it.

Through the ages volcanoes, ocean slides, the constant washing of waves, and winds have made changes in the earth's surface, so that the onetime land bridges between continents have disappeared. The land that formed the bridges sank below the surface.

It is believed that North America was once joined with Asia; Great Britain was joined with Europe; and Spain and Italy were joined with North Africa. Australia was joined to Asia. Early people, animals, and plant seeds crossed over these land bridges before the bridges disappeared beneath the sea.

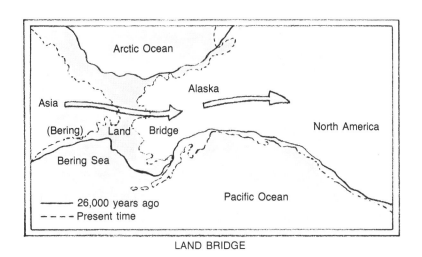

LAND BRIDGE

225 million years ago (Permian Age)

Inventions for Learning About the Sea

Since men first looked over the oceans they have wanted to know more about the parts they couldn't see. But for a long time all they could do was wonder. Of course they could swim in the edges of the oceans and pick up shells, plants, and rocks that washed ashore. They could ride over the water in boats of different kinds. But they couldn't get down into the deep parts to learn much about what was there.

But now, many new inventions have helped people find out what's under the sea. They have learned more in the last fifty years or so, than had been known since time began. But there is still much to be learned.

Men and women who study the seas are called oceanographers, or ocean scientists. There are many oceanographers all over the world. They go to schools where they learn more about our oceans, and the use of instruments made for finding out ocean secrets. They even discover ways for people to work on the ocean floor.

Oceanographers can now tell the shape of land beneath the seas, or all the ups and downs of the ocean's bottom.

Early explorers of the oceans had to use long ropes or wire cables with weights at the end to find out how deep the waters were. They dropped the ropes and weights overboard and when the weight reached the bottom, the explorers could pull them back to the ship and measure how far down they had gone. Of course they couldn't measure any more distance than the length of the ropes. In many places the ropes were not long enough or strong enough to reach bottom.

Now with sonal equipment, ships use Fathometers to send out sound signals toward the ocean's bottom. Men can tell how deep an object is below them by the length of time it takes an echo to return to the ship.

Bathyscaphes—wonderfully made research vessels with scientific instruments—along with submarines that are constantly being improved, can now be sent to great depths. They are used to bring back valuable information of the sea's wonders. It is possible that in the years to come many people will be able to use inventions not yet thought of to go to the deepest parts of an ocean.

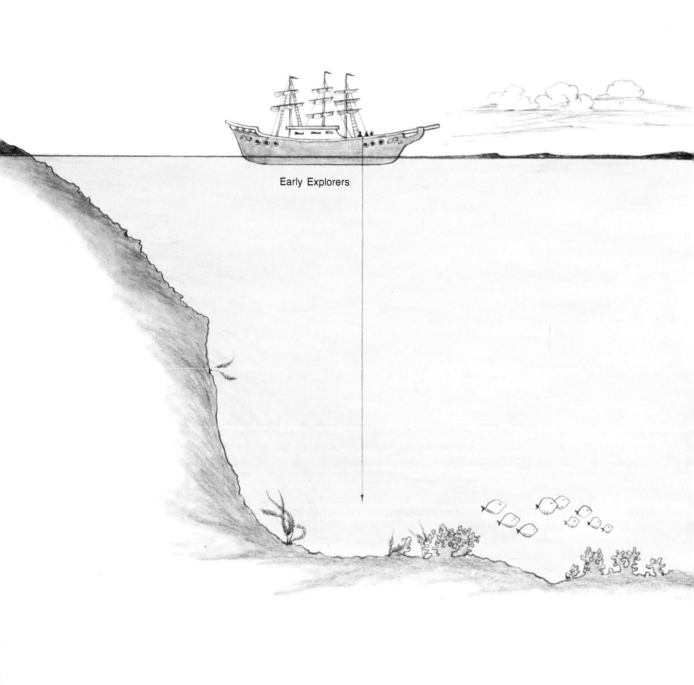

Early Explorers

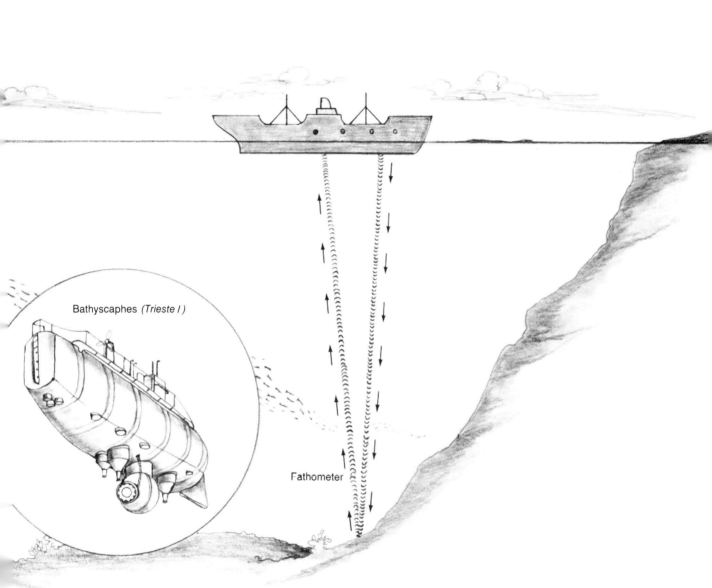

Bathyscaphes *(Trieste I)*

Fathometer

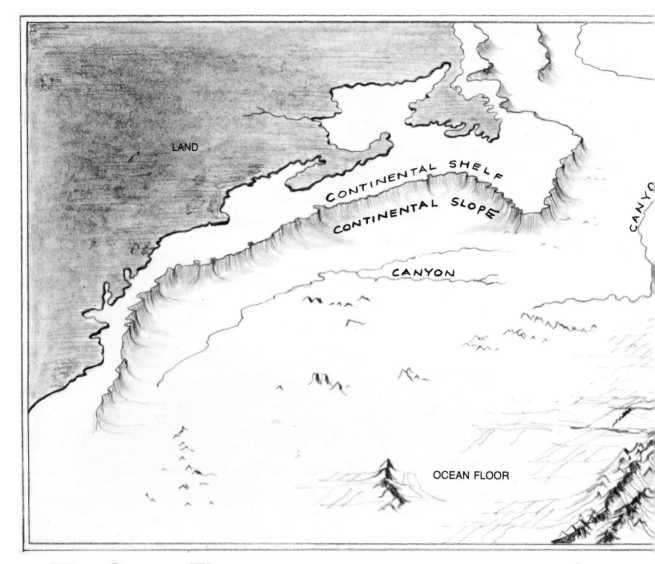

LAND

CONTINENTAL SHELF

CONTINENTAL SLOPE

CANYON

CANYON

OCEAN FLOOR

The Ocean Floor

For a long time people believed that the floor of the ocean was mostly a large, flat space. By using echo sounders, they learned that this is not true. Now much of the ocean floor has

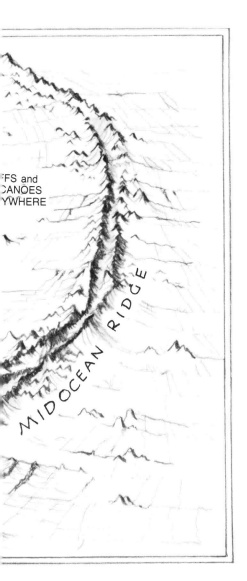

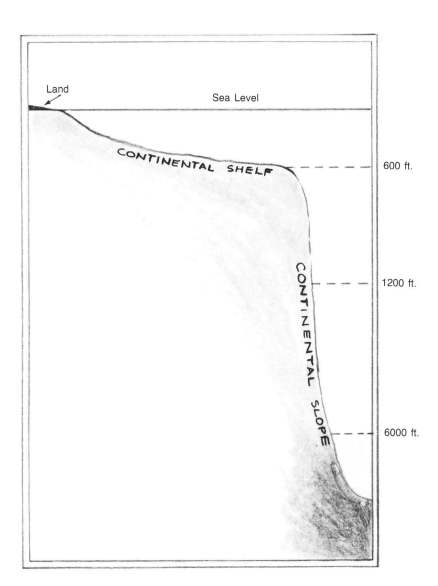

been mapped, and we know that it has mountains, deep canyons and cliffs, as well as some more-or-less flat places.

The shallowest part of the oceans is the underwater land that is just off the shores. It is called the continental shelf. It usually slopes gently from the shores to a depth of about five hundred feet.

At the seaward edge of the continental shelf the ocean floor drops sharply, going down at a steep slant for two or three miles. Where mountains are close to the shores the falloff can be as much as five miles deep.

At the bottom of the steep slopes is the deep ocean floor proper, an area that makes up half of all the earth's surface. In recent years scientists have found amazing surprises on the floor. They have found very old steep and deep canyons and ragged craggy mountains. Mounds and banks that may once have been part of land masses have somehow become part of the ocean's floor. There are volcanoes and places where heat from the hot center of the earth seeps to the surface of the ocean floor.

Perhaps the greatest discovery of all so far is that of the Midocean Ridge which was not known for certain until after World War II. In 1956 two scientists, Maurice Ewing and Bruce C. Heegan, believed that this deep-sea ridge of mountains would be found in a continuous line wherever earthquakes occurred on the ocean floor. They were right.

Now oceanograhers have learned that the Midocean Ridge is 10,000 miles long and is from 300 to 1,200 miles wide, taking up a third of the ocean bottom. It has many live volcanoes along its length. A v-shaped crevice, or rift, runs all along the top of this huge mountain chain.

The ocean floor is a vast area of mountains, trenches, plains, volcanoes, and deep holes such as the Mariana Trench, which is 6 miles deep.

Movement of the Seas, Winds, Currents, and Tides

The sea is never still. On the surface the water is constantly moving. Waves dip and roll and break in never-ending movement. Most of this surface movement is caused by the force of winds that blow over the water.

Strange as it may seem, there are large rivers running within the ocean waters. The streams flowing constantly in the seas are called currents. We can see tiny currents when we stir water with a spoon. The spoon pushes a path of water ahead of itself. When we blow across a dish of water we can see the liquid move before our breath.

Currents are caused by the way our earth spins as it makes its journey in space around the sun each day. As the earth rotates around its axis, the sun's rays strike it most directly at the equator so the water there becomes warmer than the water elsewhere. Waters at the North and South Poles, farther from the sun, are cold. When water is hot, it expands and becomes lighter. The sun-warmed water moves toward the cold water at the Poles. The heavier cold water of the Poles sinks and flows slowly toward the equator. As the water moves the rotation of the earth makes it twist around slightly so it does not move in

a straight line. This movement of hot and cold waters makes the currents, or rivers, that run in the oceans.

The winds, too, are formed in much the same way. The air is heated by the sun's rays at the equator and the rotation of the earth. The hot air rises and flows toward the Poles where it is cooled. The cool air then flows toward the equator. Strong winds, constantly blowing over the water, move currents on the surface of the seas.

In addition to the ocean movements caused by the winds and currents, there are those made by the tides. Twice each day all the seas of the world are pulled upon by a strange force from the moon and the sun called gravity. The moon's pull on the oceans is greater than that of the sun, because the moon is closer to the earth than the sun is.

At high tide the water moves upon the beaches, and at low tide it seems to run out to sea. When a tide is very low, part of the shores are uncovered for a time, and people can see into the tide pools that are usually covered with water. Sometimes tides are so high that they damage buildings and other things along the ocean's edge.

Great waves, sometimes wrongly called tidal waves, occasionally sweep over the ocean. Their true name is tsunamis *(soo-NAHM-ees)*. These tremendous waves have nothing to do with tides. They are caused by earthquakes under the sea. The force of the earthquakes makes a big push of water above itself on the surface. This becomes a huge wave that can travel as much as five hundred miles an hour. When it reaches a shore, the wave breaks with great force on land.

Tsunamis can do tremendous damage on shore. Sometimes they wash away whole towns and kill people. In 1896 a most destructive tsunami crashed along a hundred-mile coast of Japan. It killed thousands of people and washed away a great many houses.

Now scientists have tools to tell them when earthquakes occur and where they are. People can be warned of approaching tsunamis, so lives and property can be saved.

Life in the Seas

When considering things that live in the sea, oceanographers divide the sea's depth into layers, something like the layers of a cake.

The top layer is the tidal zone, the upper part of the water that is moved by the tides. The second layer is just below the tidal zone and includes the shallow seas around continents for about five hundred feet down. In these first two layers live most of the sea plants and creatures. There are many billions of these, some so small they can't be seen without a microscope. Some are so large they weigh tons.

Among the most interesting creatures in the first layer of the oceans are the bottom dwellers. They live in the sand and mud just offshore where the water is shallow. They are sluggish

sea cucumber

sea grape

sea pea

slow creatures with hard outer coverings that protect them from the pounding of the surf.

Some of these seem more like plants than animals, and some even have plantlike names, such as sea cucumbers, sea grapes, and sea peaches.

The water all about them is filled with tiny bits of food. It is made up of decaying matter and small forms of other food. So the slow bottom dwellers do not need to move about much. The food is all about them. In fact, they are really living in a kind of food soup.

Some, like the sponges, sea squirts, oysters, and clams, stay in one place and simply pump

clams

oysters

sea squirts

sponges

barnacles

the food-laden water in and out of their bodies. Parts of their bodies strain the food from the water that surrounds them. Other bottom dwellers are a little more lively. Barnacles catch bits of food with the bristle on their legs and push it into their mouths. Sea cucumbers snuff along the bottom and use their tentacles to shove slime into their mouths. Some sea cucumbers move as much as a foot and a half a day.

Sea anemones have tentacles that look like beautiful flower petals when they are feeding. The anemones wave the tentacles gently in the water and when they find food the tentacles close about the food and crush it. Anemones can catch very small fish this way. At the base of their bodies are disks that enable them to cling to rocks or move about slowly.

anemones

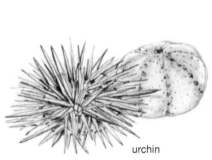

urchin

starfish

Other bottom dwellers include sea urchins, starfish, sand dollars, limpets, crabs, mussels, and whelks. Some bottom dwellers can change color so that they blend with their surroundings and cannot be easily seen.

Sometimes when we go to the beaches we see bits of lifeless shells or parts of these bottom creatures that have washed ashore.

whelk

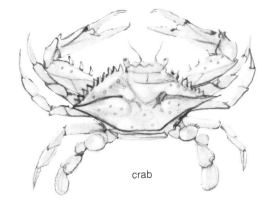

crab

mussels

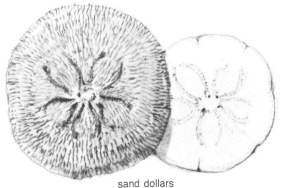

sand dollars

limpets

blue marlin

sailfish

The free-swimming sea creatures in the second zone of the ocean dash and glide through the waters. The greatest numbers of these are fish that have backbones.

Sea creatures are held up or supported by the water at all times. Unlike land creatures, they have no need for legs to keep them right-side-up. Fish are shaped to move through

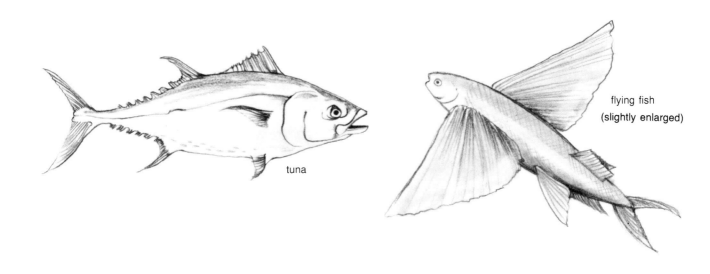

tuna

flying fish
(slightly enlarged)

water with speed by the use of their fins and tails. Some of them are very fast. The blue marlin can swim at a speed of fifty miles an hour. Other fish speedsters include sailfish, flying fish, and tuna.

In the ocean world it pays to be fast, for all the ocean creatures live by eating those smaller than themselves—ones that can't get away before being caught.

Other free-swimmers include squid, octopuses, walrus, seals, and, of course, the great whales which are the largest sea animals and the largest of other animals too.

A squid is a strange creature with ten snakelike arms, or tentacles, two of which are longer than the others. The

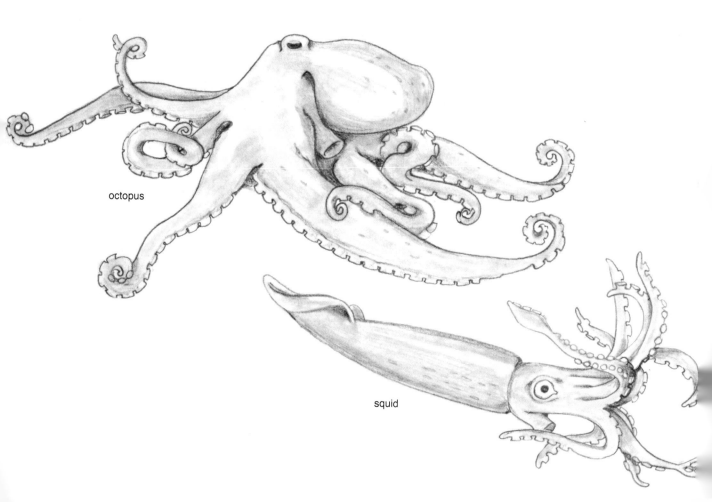

octopus

squid

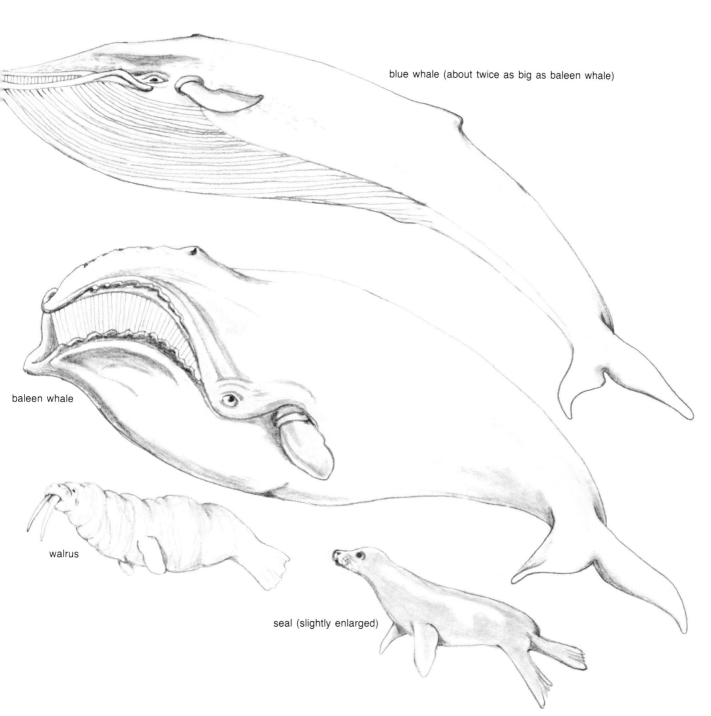

blue whale (about twice as big as baleen whale)

baleen whale

walrus

seal (slightly enlarged)

tentacles surround a mouth on the end of its torpedo-shaped body. The arms have rows of round sucker disks on them. Squid arms grasp food and the sucker disks hold the food until the twisting arms get it to the mouth. The mouth has a sharp beak like that of a parrot. Squids use the beak to tear their food apart.

The giant squid can grow to be very large and powerful—to lengths of fifty feet or more. Their tentacles can be as thick as a man's leg and the holding power of its suckers is very great.

The octopuses have eight arms or tentacles. The tentacles of some octopuses are only a few inches long. Others have tentacles so long they can spread them as far as thirty feet. All have pouch-shaped bodies with no shell. Like the squids, octopuses have suction-cup suckers on their arms.

When an octopus senses danger, it has a very good way of defending itself. It simply squirts out a cloud of inky fluid from its body and hides in the darkness of the fluid.

Both squids and octopuses can crawl about, but when they want to go fast they shoot powerful streams of water from an opening in their bodies and jet forward with their tentacles trailing in streamers behind them.

Among the thousands of different creatures that live in the seas perhaps the whales are the most interesting. Whales are not fish, they are warm-blooded mammals. And like us, they must breathe air into their lungs. The baby whale is fed with milk from its mother's body.

Blue whales are the largest animals in the world today. Perhaps they are the largest that have ever lived. When fully grown the blue whale can be a hundred feet long and weigh a hundred and fifty tons.

There are two main types of whales—those with teeth that feed mostly on squid—and those that have no teeth but have baleen in their mouths. Baleen is made up of horny plates with stiff bristles that hang from the upper jaws on each side of the baleen whales' big mouths. Baleen is commonly called whalebone.

Baleen whales swim with their mouths open and so get large quantities of water in their mouths. The whalebone plates act as strainers. They strain out the small food in the water and the whales' tongues move the food down their throats.

For many years both kinds of whales were hunted by men for the oil that is in their bodies. Whale oil is used to make products such as soap, lubricating oil, paint, and many other things.

So many whales have been killed there is great danger that they may disappear from the earth. Now most countries of the world have laws to limit the number of whales that can be killed, so that these animals can be saved for the future.

The third zone of the sea in the scientists' division is known as the zone of light. It is about six hundred feet deep and has only enough light for some things to be seen, but the light is dim.

Under this third zone—deep down in the sea—is the zone of darkness. The fish that live in the dark zone are much fewer in number than those in the light. These live only on bits of food that drift downward to the dark ocean floor and upon one another.

The dark-zone fish are different in looks from other fish. They are usually dark red, brown, or black except for some shrimps that are red or purple for no apparent reason. The deep fish are not powerful swimmers because their skeletons and muscles are not heavy enough. So, to make up for this, they, like

angler fish

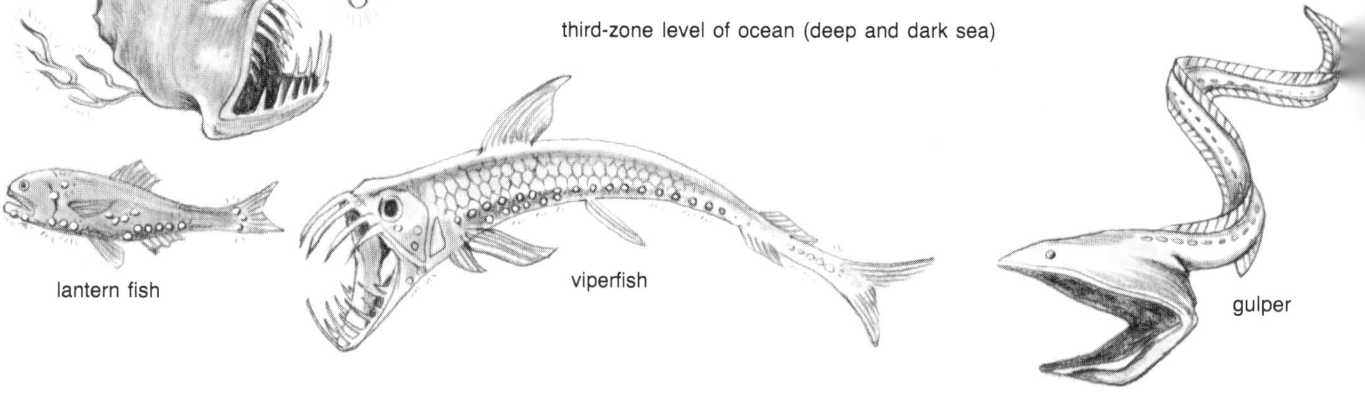

third-zone level of ocean (deep and dark sea)

lantern fish

viperfish

gulper

the gulper and viperfish, have unusually large mouths with long sharp teeth to help them get food. Some have stomachs that stretch so much they can swallow other fish larger than themselves.

Another strange thing about these deep-water fish is that many of them shine. They are lighted, or luminous. Some, like the lantern fish, have rows of light over them, arranged in patterns. Others such as angler fish have lights like torches that grow from the top of their heads. Still others have a bit of glowing light held out in front of them.

Though few of us have ever seen the strange lights of the dark-sea creatures, we have seen the tiny land beetles called fireflies that make sparks with their bodies on summer nights.

When we think of plants most of us think of the kind that grows in our gardens and fields. They have green leaves, flowers, and fruits. The plant life of the sea is quite different.

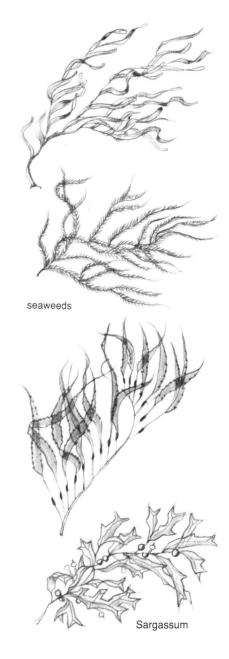

seaweeds

Sargassum

Plants cannot grow without light, so they grow only in the upper layers of the sea, mostly around the edges. They are commonly known as seaweed. Seaweed can be so small it is hard to see, or as large as the giant kelp which sometimes has strands as much as a hundred feet long. These plants can be seen among rocks at low tide.

Seaweed does not have roots or stems or flowers as land plants do. But they vary in many ways. Some are like ferns, some are like huge fans, or like vines. Many have air bladders, or air bumps, that hold them up so they can float. They are green, bluegreen, red, or brown. Large seaweeds are eaten by people in some parts of the world. The Japanese are among those who harvest seaweed for food.

One weed is the Sargassum (*Sar-GAS-sum*) weed. It has been described as grapes floating on the water. Sargassum weeds float in such huge masses in parts of the sea that ships have trouble getting through them. One such place in the Atlantic Ocean is called the Sargasso Sea.

The smallest of all sea plants are the diatoms (*dy-a-toms*). They are so small they can be seen only with a microscope. Each tiny bit has a case of clear material around it. When seen under a microscope diatoms have fantastic and beautiful shapes.

Diatoms, along with tiny animal life, make up plankton. The bits of animal and plant life in plankton are so small and weak that all they can do is drift wherever sea movements take them. In the spring huge patches of floating plankton color the surface water.

The smallest fish eat plankton and so do tiny shrimp creatures called krill. Krill is the main food of the baleen whales. Plankton has well been called the prime food supply of the sea. It is eaten by very small sea life, which in turn is eaten by larger forms of sea life, from the smallest to the largest. This arrangement of creatures always eating others smaller than themselves is often called a food chain.

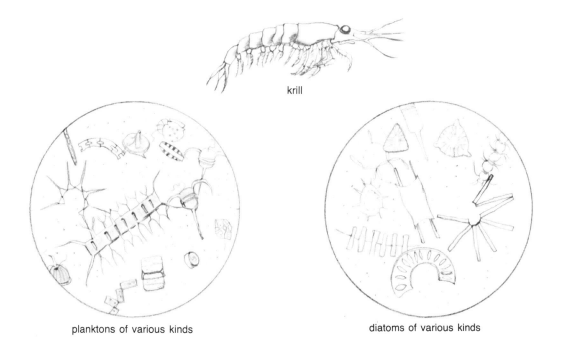

krill

planktons of various kinds

diatoms of various kinds

Non-Living Things Beneath the Sea

A great number of things that are not alive are beneath the sea. Ever since boats have been used, some have been wrecked and sunk to the bottom of the water. The sea is a graveyard for wrecked ships.

Divers for years have brought up all kinds of things—dishes, urns, silver, gold, statues, carvings, furnishings of many kinds—that they found in old shipwrecks.

Ancient cities, too, that were destroyed by earthquakes, lie in ruins on the seas' bottom, covered with mud and sand. The ruins of these are fascinating to divers. They are also fascinating to people who are interested in the past and want to know more about people who lived centuries ago.

Among the men who have worked undersea and have invented things like bathyscaphes, and other underwater vessels, and submarines, and ways to learn more about sunken treasures, the name of Jacques-Yves Cousteau is well-known. Cousteau and Émile Gagnan of France together developed and patented (1947) the underwater breathing apparatus called the AquaLung, or scuba. With it divers can move underwater breathing the air they carry in their tanks. They can investigate and find treasures of the sea that would be impossible to find without the use of this important invention.

A number of other men have also made machines, diving suits, scientific instruments, and numerous other things that make possible the work of discovering what has lain on the ocean floor unknown for hundreds of years. Now, on television, we can often see live pictures of people at work finding out more about the sea's hidden treasures.

The Future

Truly the seas are full of treasures. Those that come from sunken ships and cities of long ago are only a small part of the ocean's wealth. The ocean is a storehouse of food. Fish and other food from the sea will be in greater use in the future, it is believed. We are learning better ways of using and producing it and being careful that sea life will not disappear.

The huge amounts of minerals in the ocean and on the ocean floor can be used in countless ways as we learn more about them and about how to reclaim them. These include gold, silver, copper, aluminum, magnesium, uranium, and manganese. All of these are useful in industry for our modern ways of living.

Oil from wells driven into the ocean floor is wealth that we will get more of as exploring continues.

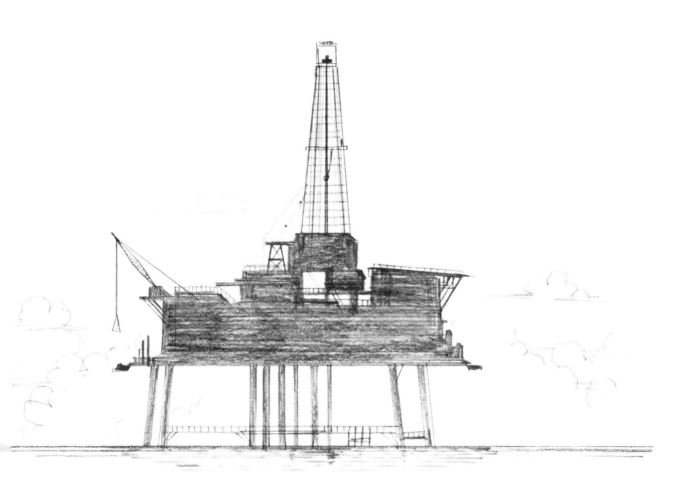

oil well

The ocean water is salty, so salty that it has had few uses in modern life. But now there are ways of removing the salt, and new and better ways are being developed. It seems possible that in the future salt can be taken from ocean water so that the water will be fresh. Then it can be pumped to areas to be used for growing crops and for other fresh-water needs. It is also possible that in the future water from fresh-water springs on the bottom of the ocean can be piped through the salt water to land.

Oceanographers believe that we are just beginning to find out how to use the oceans for many discoveries and for uses that we cannot yet imagine. They feel certain that the future will be better in many ways through the use of what's under the sea.

GLOSSARY

AXIS   The imaginary line around which the earth spins

BALEEN   Horny plates in the mouths of baleen whales used to strain food from ocean water—often called whalebone

BATHYSPHERE   A diving bell or ball for research, lowered into the water by cables

CONTINENTAL SHELF   The land under water just off the shores of earth

COUSTEAU, JACQUES-YVES   *(Koo-stoh, Jahk-Eve)* Famous underwater explorer and inventor of AquaLung and diving gear

CURRENTS   Streams of water running within oceans

DIATOM   Exceedingly small sea plants that can be seen only with a microscope

ECHO SOUNDER   Machine for finding out distances that can't be easily measured—sends out and receives sound pulses

EQUATOR   Place around the earth that is equally distant from the North and South Poles

FATHOMETER   A device for measuring depth of water

GRAVITY   The strange pulling power exerted by the moon and sun upon our earth

LUMINOUS   Shining

MARIANA TRENCH   Deepest place known in the ocean

INDEX